How many bead

● Count up to 100 objects by grouping th

꿰 ꘯꘯ ꘯꘯ ꘯꘯ ꘯꘯ ꘯꘯ ꘯꘯ III   **23**

Teacher's notes

How many beads are there in each necklace? On the line next to each necklace make a tally mark for
each bead. Group the tally marks in fives and write the total number of beads in the box.

3

Date _____

Greater than, less than

- Compare numbers up to 100
- Use the greater than (>) and less than (<) signs

Teacher's notes

4

Write a number or the <, > or = symbol in the spaces so that each number sentence is correct.

Date _____

Rounding the sheep

● **Round numbers less than 100 to the nearest 10**

Teacher's notes
Draw a line to match each sheep to the shepherd which shows the sheep's number rounded to the nearest ten.

Date _____

Air balloon estimates

● Estimate numbers up to 100 and place them on a number line

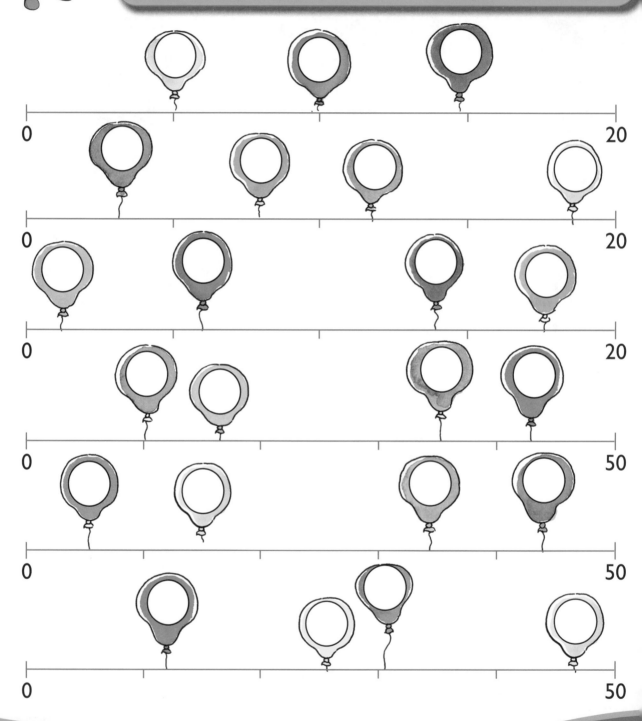

Teacher's notes

Look at the position of the balloons on each number line. Estimate the position of the balloons by writing the appropriate number on each one.

Date _____

Archery addition

Add more than two numbers

$4 + 9 + 2 = 15$

Teacher's notes
Work out the score on each target and write your calculation in the box underneath.

Addition 100

Date_____

● Begin to add three two-digit numbers

You need:
● coloured pencils

1	2	3	4	5	6	7	8	9	10
11	12	13	14	15	16	17	18	19	20
21	22	23	24	25	26	27	28	29	30
31	32	33	34	35	36	37	38	39	40
41	42	43	44	45	46	47	48	49	50
51	52	53	54	55	56	57	58	59	60
61	62	63	64	65	66	67	68	69	70
71	72	73	74	75	76	77	78	79	80
81	82	83	84	85	86	87	88	89	90
91	92	93	94	95	96	97	98	99	100

7 + 19 + 20 = 46   ◯ + ◯ + ◯ = 79

◯ + ◯ + ◯ = 58   ◯ + ◯ + ◯ = 84

◯ + ◯ + ◯ = 63   ◯ + ◯ + ◯ = 92

Teacher's notes

8

For each calculation, find three numbers in the one hundred square which give the total.
Then colour each of the numbers to match the colour of the total.

Date _____

Car calculations

- Understand that subtraction 'undoes' addition

You need:
- coloured pencils

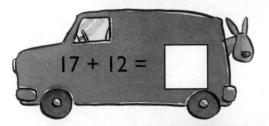

17 + 12 =

38 − 25

21 + 14 =

47 − 19

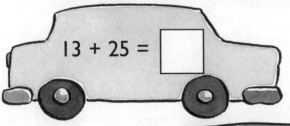

13 + 25 =

49 − 21

23 + 24 =

29 − 12

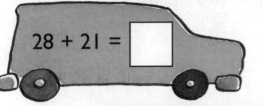

28 + 21 =

35 − 14

47 − 24

19 + 28 =

Teacher's notes

Complete the addition calculations on the cars and the subtraction calculations on the petrol pumps.
Colour the subtraction petrol pump calculation to match the corresponding addition car calculation.

9

Date_____

Addition addresses

● Add 19 and 21 by adding 20 and adjusting by 1

Teacher's notes

Add 19 and 21 to the number shown on the door. Draw a line to the two children showing the correct answers. Colour the 'add 19' child's shirt yellow and the 'add 21' child's shirt blue.

10

Date_____

Holiday shopping

● **Solve problems about money**

40p

10p

20p

15p

 Samira had 50p to spend.

She bought a and

[ ] p + [ ] p = [ ] p

How much change did Samira have left?

[ ] p − [ ] p = [ ] p

 Tom had 50p to spend.

He bought a and

[ ] p + [ ] p = [ ] p

How much change did Tom have left?

[ ] p − [ ] p = [ ] p

 Ellis had 60p to spend.

He bought 4

[ ] p × [ ] = [ ] p

How much change did Ellis have left?

[ ] p − [ ] p = [ ] p

Holly had 60p to spend.
She bought a

She used 4 identical coins to pay.
How much was each coin worth?

[ ] p ÷ [ ] = [ ] p

How much change did Holly have left?

[ ] p − [ ] p = [ ] p

Teacher's notes

Using addition, subtraction, multiplication and division calculations, first work out how much each child spent and how much money they had left.

Date _____

Magic numbers

● **Know pairs of numbers with a total of 20 and 100**

Teacher's notes

In the spaces provided, write your own calculations to show pairs of numbers totalling 20 in the top cauldron, and multiples of 10 totalling 100 in the bottom cauldron.

Date _____

Subtraction soccer

● **Know the subtraction facts to 10**

 8 − 5
 9 − 4
 10 − 4
 9 − 2
 6 − 4
 10 − 1

 1
 2
 6
 7
 10

 3
 4
 5
 8
 9

 8 − 7
 4 − 2
 9 − 1
 9 − 5
 7 − 2
 10 − 0

Teacher's notes

Work out the subtraction calculation on each player's shirt then draw a line to the ball showing the correct answer.

13

Date_____

Shopping multiples

● Begin to recognise numbers to 100 that are multiples of 2, 5 or 10

Multiples of 2	Multiples of 5	Multiples of 10	Others
12p			
20p			
24p			

Teacher's notes

14

Decide whether the price on each item is a multiple of 2, 5 or 10. Write each number on the appropriate shopping bill. Some prices can go on more than one bill.

Date _____

Bugs together

● **Describe patterns and relationships**

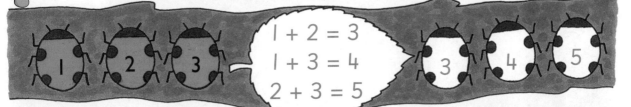

1 + 2 = 3
1 + 3 = 4
2 + 3 = 5

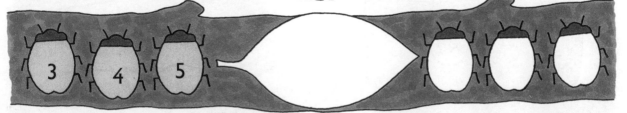

Teacher's notes
On each branch, add the numbers on the first three bugs in pairs. Write your working-out on the leaf.
Then write the answers on the last three bugs, from smallest to largest.

15

Date _____

Sausage puzzles

● Solve puzzles

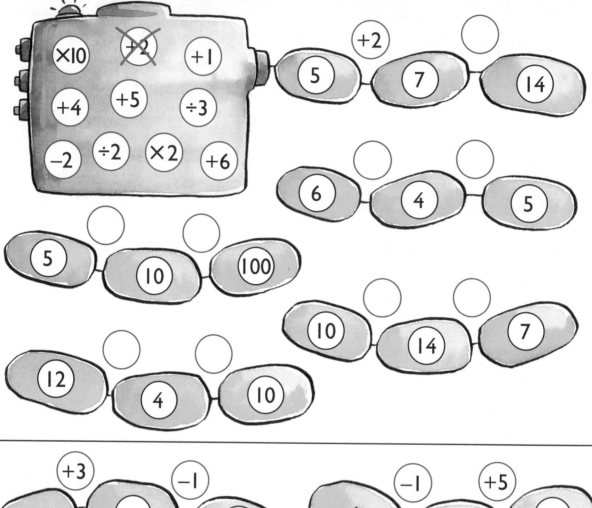

Teacher's notes

Top: Look at the numbers on each string of sausages and choose the appropriate number operations from the sausage machine. Write the operations in the circles.

Bottom: Using the operations, complete the calculations by writing the missing numbers on the sausages.

Date _____

Half-time halves and doubles

● **Understand that halving is the opposite of doubling**

$7 \times 2 =$ ☐

12

$6 \times 2 =$ ☐

$12 \div 2 = 6$

14

☐ $\div 2 = 7$

$8 \times 2 =$ ☐

20

☐ $\div 2 = 8$

☐ $\div 2 = 10$

16

$10 \times 2 =$ ☐

Teacher's notes

Complete the calculations on each footballer then draw a line from the multiplication and division calculations to the football that shows the 'missing' number for each.

17

Date _____

Dinosaur facts

● **Know the 2 and 10 times tables and the related division facts**

$4 \times 2 = \boxed{8}$

$\boxed{8} \div \boxed{2} = \boxed{4}$

$5 \times 2 = \boxed{}$

$\boxed{} \div \boxed{} = \boxed{}$

$3 \times 10 = \boxed{}$

$\boxed{} \div \boxed{} = \boxed{}$

$7 \times 2 = \boxed{}$

$\boxed{} \div \boxed{} = \boxed{}$

$5 \times 10 = \boxed{}$

$\boxed{} \div \boxed{} = \boxed{}$

Teacher's notes

18

On each pair of dinosaurs, first complete the multiplication calculations in the spaces provided, then write the corresponding division calculation.

Date_____

Fizzy fives

● **Know the 5 times table and the related division facts**

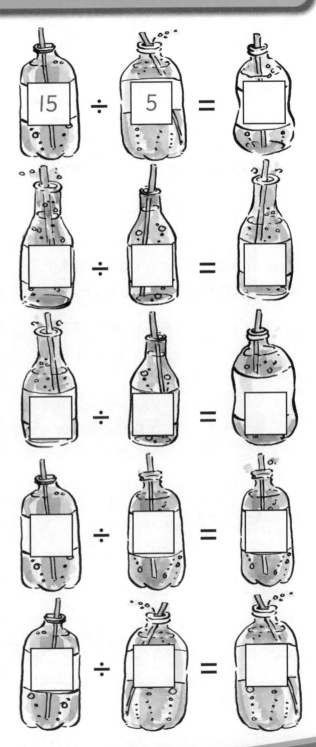

$3 \times 5 =$ | 15 | 15 ÷ 5 = ⬜

$7 \times 5 =$

$5 \times 5 =$

$9 \times 5 =$

$8 \times 5 =$

Teacher's notes

On each set of bottles, first complete the multiplication calculation in the spaces provided, then write the corresponding division calculation.

19

Date _____

What's the problem?

● **Solve word problems**

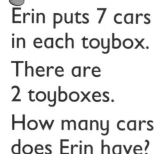

Erin puts 7 cars in each toybox.
There are 2 toyboxes.
How many cars does Erin have?

 × =

She finds 3 more cars under her bed! Now, how many cars?

 + =

Ellis bakes 20 biscuits.
He eats 4 of them.
How many are left?

 ○ ○

He shares these between 2 friends. How many biscuits does each friend have?

 ○ ○

Malkeet buys 5 pencils for 5p each.
How much does he spend?

 ○ ○

How much change does he get from 40p?

Kaya shares 18 flowers between 3 vases.
How many flowers in each vase?

 ○ ○

She puts 5 more flowers into each vase. How many has she added?

Teacher's notes

Read each two-step word problem and complete the number sentences to find the correct answers.

Date_____

Car calculations

● **Solve word problems about division**

11 passengers travel in 3 cars.

How many in each car?

15 passengers travel in 2 cars.

How many in each car?

19 passengers travel in 4 cars.

How many in each car?

25 passengers travel in 7 cars.

How many in each car?

Teacher's notes

Work out the answer to each of the division word problems and write the complete calculation on the car next to each one. Then join the car to the petrol pump showing the correct remainder.

21

Date_____

All about 2-D shapes

● **Name and describe 2-D shapes**

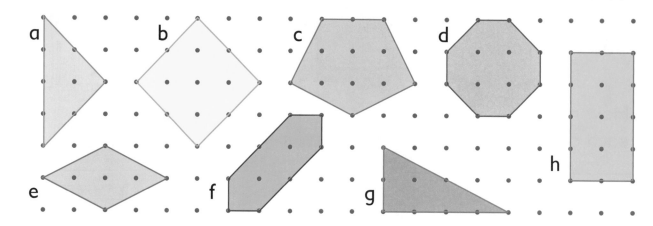

Shape	all sides the same length	5 or more corners	1 or more right angles
a	✗	✗	✓
b			
c			
d			
e			
f			
g			
h			

One of the shapes is not symmetrical. Write its letter.

Teacher's notes

22

Look at the sides, corners and angles in each shape. Complete the table. Put a ✓ for yes and a ✗ for no.
Find which shape does not have a line of symmetry.

Date _____

Patterns and puzzles

You need:
● coloured pencils   ● ruler

● **Describe and continue the pattern for a set of shapes**

Repeating bead patterns

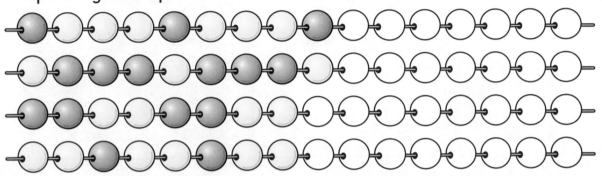

Repeating shape patterns

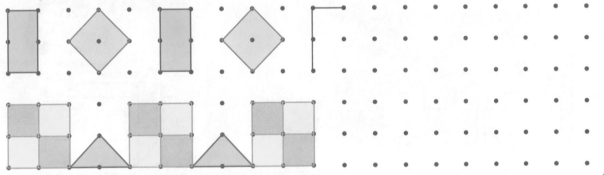

Shape puzzle

| 3 | rectangles

☐ rectangles

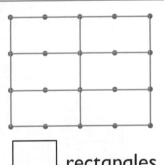

☐ rectangles

Teacher's notes

Top and middle: Continue the bead and shape patterns as far as you can go.
Bottom: Count the number of rectangles in each diagram and write the answer in the box.

23

Date_____

All about 3-D solids

● **Count the number of faces, sides and corners of 3-D solids**

Count the faces

Count the corners

Count the edges

Teacher's notes

Top: For each shape, count the number of faces and write the answer in the square.
Middle: Find the number of corners for each shape and write the answer in the square.
Bottom: Write the number of edges in the square for each shape.

Date_____

Bus tour times

● **Decide which calculations you need to solve a problem involving time**

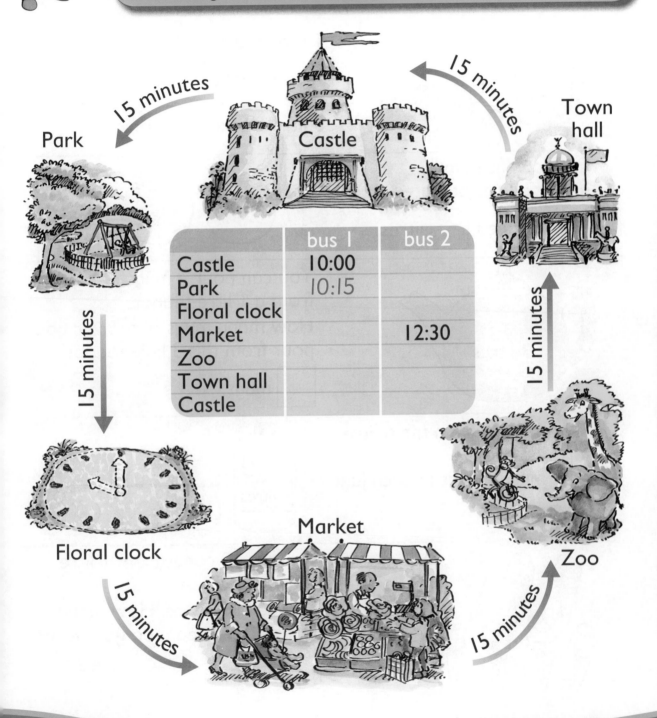

Park

Castle

Town hall

15 minutes

15 minutes

15 minutes

15 minutes

	bus 1	bus 2
Castle	10:00	
Park	10:15	
Floral clock		
Market		12:30
Zoo		
Town hall		
Castle		

Floral clock

Market

Zoo

15 minutes

15 minutes

Teacher's notes

The two circular bus tours of the city begin at the castle. The buses take 15 minutes between each place of interest. Complete the timetable for the two tour buses.

Date_____

Fete Day problems

● **Decide which calculation you need to solve a problem involving litres**

1 litre makes 5 drinks.

2 litres make ☐ drinks.

3 litres make ☐ drinks.

Each goldfish bowl
needs 2 litres of water.

4 bowls need ☐ litres.

3 litres

You can pour 4 mugs of tea
from a 1 litre teapot.

How many mugs of tea will you
pour from this 3 litre teapot?

☐ mugs

Fill the 3 jugs from the 6 litre
carton of milk.
How much milk is in each jug?

☐ litres

6 litres

You get 10 cones from 1 litre
tub of ice cream.

You sell 50 cones. How many
litres of ice cream do you need?

☐ litres

Teacher's notes
Read each word problem and write the answer in the box.

26

Date_____

Comparing capacities

● Compare two containers to see which holds more

1

→ B
→ A

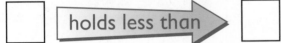

| B | holds more than | A |

| | holds less than | |

2

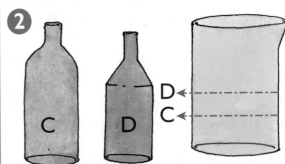

D ◄
C ◄

| | holds more than | |

| | holds less than | |

3

→ Q
→ P

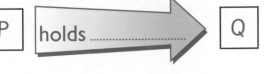

| P | holds .... | Q |

4

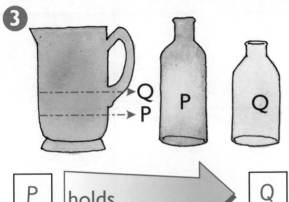

R ◄
S ◄

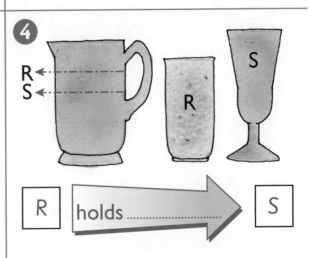

| R | holds .... | S |

5 We used the same measuring jug in questions **3** and **4**.

Container Q holds [_____] container R.

Container P holds [_____] container S.

Date_____

Looking at litres

● **Use a litre measuring jug to find out how much water other containers hold**

You need:
● 1 litre measuring jug
● funnel
● 5 different sized containers

	Holds less than 1 litre	Holds about 1 litre	Holds more than 1 litre
Container 1 is a _bottle_	✓		
Container 2 is a			
Container 3 is a			
Container 4 is a			
Container 5 is a			

Teacher's notes

28

Work in groups. Guess whether your first container will hold more, less, or about 1 litre (✓).
Draw a circle in the correct box. Pour the contents in your measuring jar. If you estimated correctly,
tick inside the circle.

Date _____

Fish tank litres

● **Read scales marked in 1s, 5s and 10s**

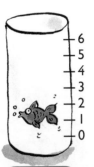 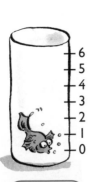  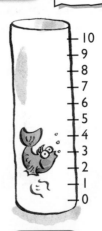 

5 litres   4 litres   7 litres   8 litres   10 litres

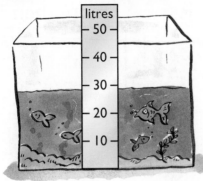

just under _____ litres

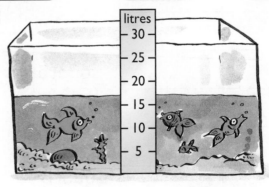

just over _____ litres

more than _____ litres

less than _____ litres

Teacher's notes

Top: Fill each jar to the number of litres shown on the label. Colour the water blue.
Bottom: In each tank, read the level of the water to the nearest whole litre.
        Write your answer in the space below.

29

Date _____

Sorting shapes and numbers

● **Sort objects and use diagrams to show how they were sorted**

4 3 11 7 16 3

2 17 16 8

13 1 1 11 10 20

20 14 15 2 13

18 15 9 12 3 19

Shape	Number

	10 or less	more than 10
square	○	○
Not square	○	○

There are ☐ triangles.

☐ squares have 10 or less.

☐ shapes are not square and have more than 10.

Teacher's notes

30 Count the number of each shape and complete the table. Then cross out each shape and make a tick in the correct set of the sorting diagram. Count the ticks and write the totals in the circles. Complete the sentences. Sort the shapes a different way using the lower diagram.

Date _____

Rabbit sorting

● **Draw a pictogram**

Rabbit sizes

Large	∨	∨	∨		
Medium					
Small					

Number of rabbits

∨

Stands for 1 rabbit

Rabbit colours

Brown					
White					
Dark Grey					

Number of rabbits

Stands for 1 rabbit

Teacher's notes

Count the small, medium and large rabbits. For each one draw ∨ in a box in the size pictogram.
Count the light brown, white and dark grey rabbits. Record the information in the colour pictogram.

31

Date _____

Seaside sorting

● **Draw a pictogram**

Clothes

Swimsuit					
Shorts					
Dress					

Number of children

Stands for 1 child

Toys

Bucket				
Spade				
Ball				
Bat				

Number of toys

Stands for 1 toy

There are ☐ children

There are ☐ toys

Teacher's notes

Count the children wearing a swimsuit, a dress or shorts. For each one, draw the picture in a box in the clothes pictogram. Now count the toys. Record the information in the toys pictogram. Complete the sentences.

Date _____

Money sorting

- Sort objects and use diagrams to show how they were sorted
- Organise information and make a pictogram

	Heads	Tails
Silver	◯	◯
Not silver	◯	◯

1p					
2p					
5p					
10p					
20p					

Number of coins

There are ☐ silver coins.

☐ silver coins are Heads.

The least common coin is ☐

Teacher's notes

Make a tick for each coin in the sorting diagram. Count the ticks and write the totals in the circles.
Then complete the pictogram. Complete the sentences.

33

Date_____

Nest sorting

● **Draw a block graph**

You need:
● coloured pencils

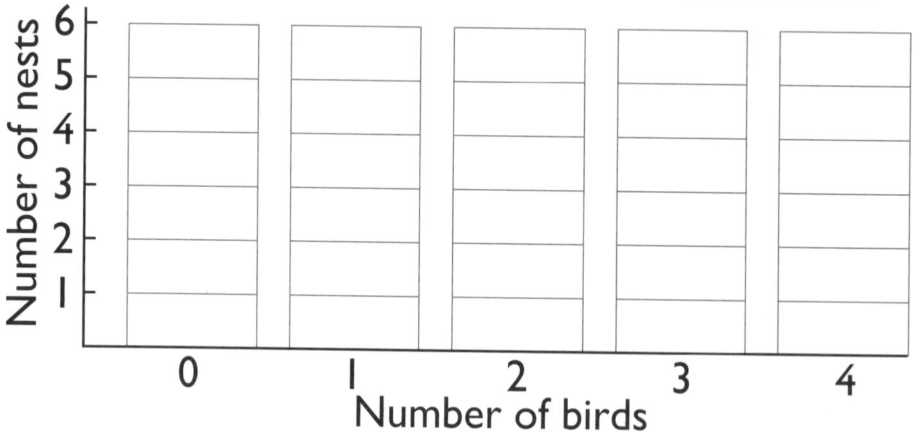

Number of nests

6
5
4
3
2
1

0   1   2   3   4

Number of birds

☐ nests have 3 birds.   ☐ nests have 2 birds.

Teacher's notes

34

Count the number of birds in each nest and record the information in the correct column.
Then complete the sentences at the bottom of the page.

Date _____

Fast food facts

● Organise information using tables, pictograms and block graphs

You need:
● coloured pencils

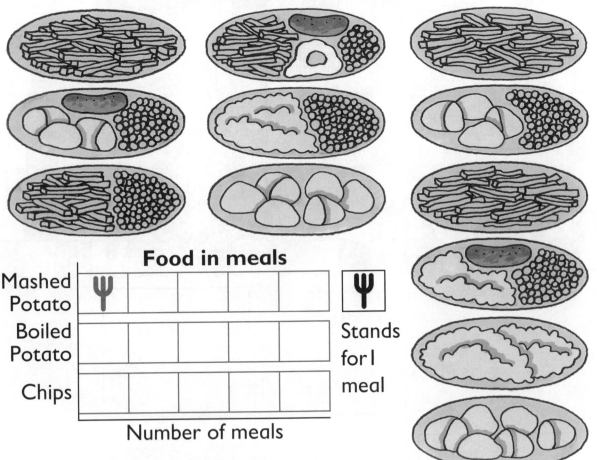

Food in meals

Mashed Potato	Ψ				
Boiled Potato					
Chips					

Number of meals

Ψ Stands for 1 meal

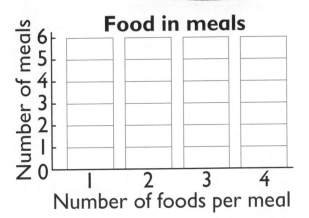

Food in meals

Food	Number of meals
1	
2	
3	
4	

Food in meals

Number of meals (6, 5, 4, 3, 2, 1, 0) vs Number of foods per meal (1, 2, 3, 4)

Teacher's notes
Look at the foods at the top of the page and complete the pictogram, table and block graph.

Date _____

Picnic sorting

● **Sort objects and make a pictogram**

Red

Plate

Colour

Number

Stands for 1 object

Teacher's notes

Make a tick for each object in the sorting diagram. Complete the pictogram.

Date _____

Bridging through 10

● **Add or subtract mentally**

Bridge

| 0 | 1 | 2 | 3 | 4 | 5 | 6 | 7 | 8 | 9 | 10 | 11 | 12 | 13 | 14 | 15 | 16 | 17 | 18 | 19 | 20 |

13 – 7

| 13 | – | 3 | – | 4 |

| 10 | – | 4 | = | 6 |

14 – 6

| ☐ | – | ☐ | – | ☐ |

| ☐ | – | ☐ | = | ☐ |

16 – 8

| ☐ | – | ☐ | – | ☐ |

| ☐ | – | ☐ | = | ☐ |

17 – 9

| ☐ | – | ☐ | – | ☐ |

| ☐ | – | ☐ | = | ☐ |

16 – 9

| ☐ | – | ☐ | – | ☐ |

| ☐ | – | ☐ | = | ☐ |

18 – 9

| ☐ | – | ☐ | – | ☐ |

| ☐ | – | ☐ | = | ☐ |

Teacher's notes
Solve each subtraction calculation by bridging through 10, using the number line to help you.

Date _____

Bridging through 20

● **Add or subtract mentally**

16 + 6

Bridge 20

| 16 | 17 | 18 | 19 | | 21 | 22 | 23 | 24 | 25 |

16 (+) 6 = 16 (+) 4 (+) 2 = 20 (+) 2 = 22

Bridge 20   **22 − 7**

| 11 | 12 | 13 | 14 | 15 | 16 | 17 | 18 | 19 | | 21 | 22 |

☐ ○ ☐ = ☐ ○ ☐ ○ ☐ = ☐ ○ ☐ = ☐

18 + 8

Bridge 20

| 18 | 19 | | 21 | 22 | 23 | 24 | 25 | 26 | 27 | 28 |

☐ ○ ☐ = ☐ ○ ☐ ○ ☐ = ☐ ○ ☐ = ☐

Bridge 20   **24 − 8**

| 14 | 15 | 16 | 17 | 18 | 19 | | 21 | 22 | 23 | 24 |

☐ ○ ☐ = ☐ ○ ☐ ○ ☐ = ☐ ○ ☐ = ☐

17 + 9

Bridge 20

| 17 | 18 | 19 | | 21 | 22 | 23 | 24 | 25 | 26 | 27 | 28 |

☐ ○ ☐ = ☐ ○ ☐ ○ ☐ = ☐ ○ ☐ = ☐

Teacher's notes

38

Work out the addition and subtraction calculations by bridging through 20.
Write the calculations in the spaces provided.

Date _____

Pyramid patterns

- **Recognise patterns in calculations**

$7 - 2 = 5$
$17 - 2 = 15$
$27 - 2 = 25$

$5 + 4 = 9$
$15 + 4 = 19$
$25 + 4 = 29$

$3 + 5 = 8$
$13 + 5 = 18$

$19 - 6 = 13$
$29 - 6 = 23$

$24 - 2 = $

Teacher's notes

Look at the calculations on each pyramid and find the pattern. Continuing with the pattern, write the other calculations on to each pyramid in the spaces provided.

39

Date _____

Summer fair solutions

● **Solve word problems**

Yasmin had 50p to spend.

She bought a plate for 20p.

☐ p ◯ ☐ p ◯ ☐ p

Then a cup for 15p.

☐ p ◯ ☐ p ◯ ☐ p

Altogether Yasmin spent

☐ p ◯ ☐ p ◯ ☐ p

Ben had 40 plants to sell. First he sold 27.

☐ ◯ ☐ ◯ ☐

Then he sold 11 more.

☐ ◯ ☐ ◯ ☐

Altogether Ben sold

☐ ◯ ☐ ◯ ☐ plants.

Lucy baked 16 cakes and Ellis baked 18.

☐ ◯ ☐ ◯ ☐

They baked ☐ cakes for the stall.

They sold 22.

☐ ◯ ☐ ◯ ☐

They had ☐ left.

Theo had 30p to spend. He spent 12p on sweets.

☐ p ◯ ☐ p ◯ ☐ p

Theo had ☐ p left.

He won 20p on Hook-a-duck.

☐ p ◯ ☐ p ◯ ☐ p

Now Theo had ☐ p altogether.

Teacher's notes

40

Look at each problem and write the calculations in the spaces provided.
Now write the answer to each problem.

Date _____

Shopping problems

● **Solve word problems**

Mr Bunn baked 50 doughnuts. 20 were jam, 16 were custard and the last were ring.

How many were ring doughnuts?

Ms Green shared 16 kg of cherries equally between 4 crates. On Monday she sold 3 crates. How many kgs of cherries did she sell?

Mr Bunn baked ⬜ ring doughnuts.

Ms Green sold ⬜ kg of cherries.

Mrs Wrench had 11 pots of paint. 14 more were delivered. She put the same number of paint pots on each of the 5 shelves. How many pots on each shelf?

Mr Pott sold 9 bunches of roses for £2 each. He also sold 3 bunches of lillies for £5 each. How much money did he make from these sales?

Mrs Wrench had ⬜ pots on each shelf.

Mr Pott made £ ⬜ from the roses and lillies.

Teacher's notes

Look at each problem and show how you work out the answer underneath.
Write the answer in the space provided.

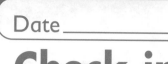

Date_____

Check-in calculations

● **Solve problems involving time**

CNPM Tours
Please check in
2 hours before
take-off time

	TAKE-OFF TIME
Florida	quarter past 12
Spain	quarter to 4
Italy	quarter past 1
Greece	half past 2

Florida

10 : 15

Greece

:

Spain

:

Italy

:

Check in time	Take-off time	
7:15	2 hours later	
8:00	5 hours later	
6:15	3 hours 15 minutes later	
7:15	2 hours 30 minutes later	

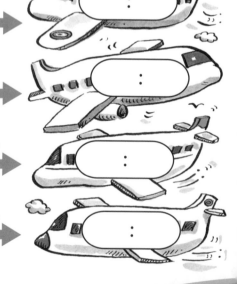

Teacher's notes

Top: The check-in times are 2 hours before each take-off time. Write the correct check-in
times on each suitcase.
Bottom: Read each problem and write the digital time on the aircraft.

Date _____

Right angle testing

● **Know that a right angle makes a quarter turn**

Teacher's notes

Test each picture for right angles. At the top, tick (✓) the pictures with any right angles.
At the bottom, mark all the right angles in each shape with a small square.

Date _____

Patterns with a quarter turn

● Use quarter turns to make a pattern

You need:
● coloured pencils

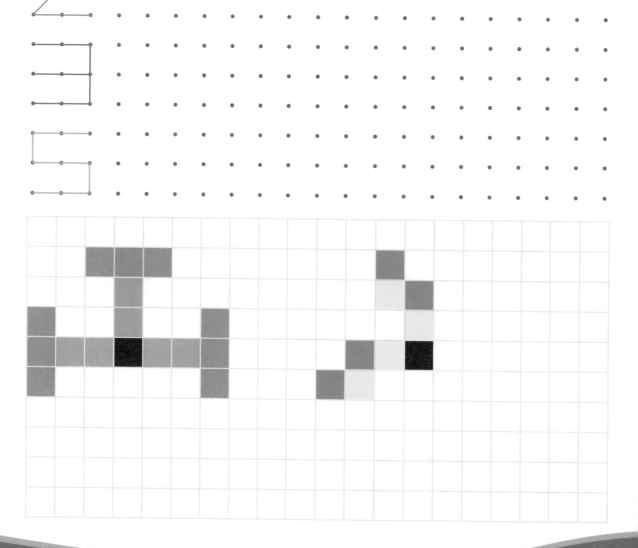

Teacher's notes

44

Top: Draw 3 more letters in each row. Turn the letter through a quarter turn each time.
Bottom: Turn the shape through a right angle each time. Complete each pattern.

Date_____

Calculating capacities

● **Read scales marked in 100 ml measures**

You need:

● coloured pencil

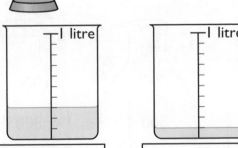

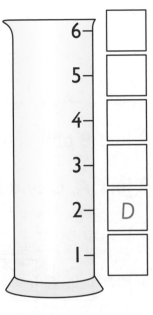

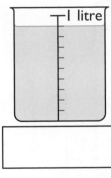

300 ml

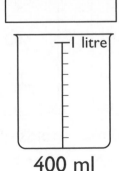

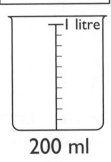

500 ml   400 ml   200 ml   800 ml

Teacher's notes

Top: Count the number of cups each container holds and write its letter on the scale.
Middle: Write how many millilitres are in each measuring jar.
Bottom: Draw a line and colour to show how much water is in each jar.

45

Date_____

Litres and millilitres

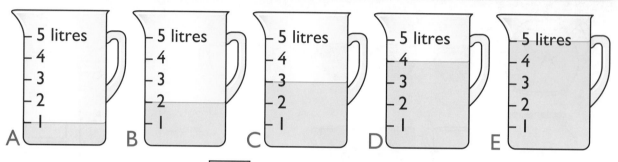

● Read scales marked in 200 ml measures
● Decide what calculation to do to solve a problem

A   B   C   D   E

① Jars B and C hold ☐ litres of water altogether.

② Jars A, D and E hold ☐ litres of water altogether.

③ If you pour ☐ litres into jar A, it will hold the same as jar E.

④ Jars ☐ , ☐ and ☐ hold 11 litres altogether.

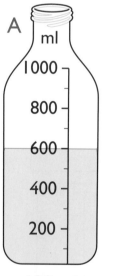

600 ml

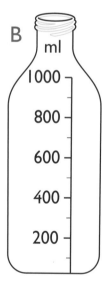

holds 200 ml
more than A

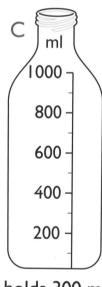

holds 300 ml
less than A

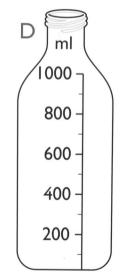

holds 400 ml
less than B

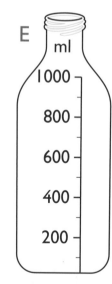

holds 500 ml
more than C

Teacher's notes

46

Top: Use the pictures of the measuring jars to solve the problems.
Bottom: Read the clue below each bottle then colour to show the level of water in the bottle.

Date _____

Multiplication facts for 2

- Know the 2 times table and the related division facts
- Recognise multiples of 2

You need:

- coloured pencils

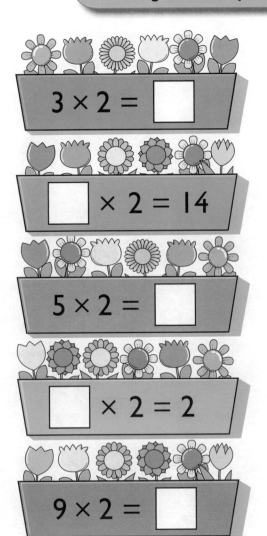

$3 \times 2 = \boxed{}$

$\boxed{} \times 2 = 14$

$5 \times 2 = \boxed{}$

$\boxed{} \times 2 = 2$

$9 \times 2 = \boxed{}$

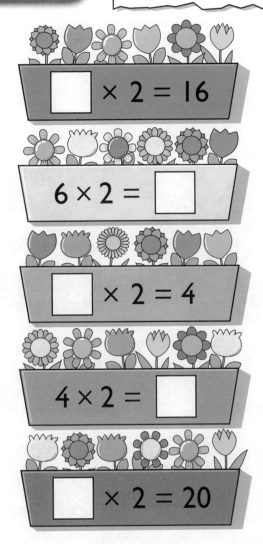

$\boxed{} \times 2 = 16$

$6 \times 2 = \boxed{}$

$\boxed{} \times 2 = 4$

$4 \times 2 = \boxed{}$

$\boxed{} \times 2 = 20$

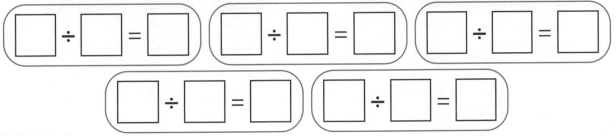

$\boxed{} \div \boxed{} = \boxed{}$ $\boxed{} \div \boxed{} = \boxed{}$ $\boxed{} \div \boxed{} = \boxed{}$

$\boxed{} \div \boxed{} = \boxed{}$ $\boxed{} \div \boxed{} = \boxed{}$

Teacher's notes

Complete each multiplication fact for 2 by writing the missing number in each space. Then choose five of these and write the related division fact for each one. Colour them to match.

47

Date _____

Multiplication facts for 5

- **Know the 5 times table and the related division facts**
- **Recognise multiples of 5**

$3 \times 5 = \boxed{}$

$\boxed{} \times 5 = 35$

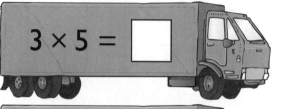

$\boxed{} \times 5 = 25$

$2 \times 5 = \boxed{}$

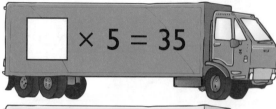

$1 \times 5 = \boxed{}$

$\boxed{} \times 5 = 20$

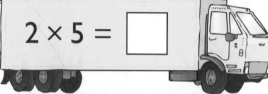

$\boxed{} \times 5 = 40$

$6 \times 5 = \boxed{}$

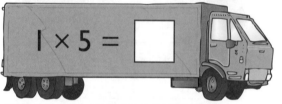

$9 \times 5 = \boxed{}$

$\boxed{} \times 5 = 50$

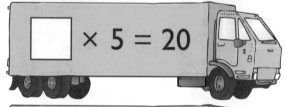
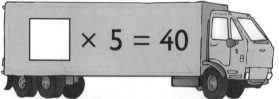

$\boxed{} \div \boxed{} = \boxed{}$ $\boxed{} \div \boxed{} = \boxed{}$ $\boxed{} \div \boxed{} = \boxed{}$

$\boxed{} \div \boxed{} = \boxed{}$ $\boxed{} \div \boxed{} = \boxed{}$

Teacher's notes

48

Complete each multiplication fact for 5 by writing the missing number into each space. Then choose five of these and write the related division fact for each one. Colour them to match.

Date_____

Multiplication facts for 10

- **Know the 10 times table and the related division facts**
- **Recognise multiples of 10**

You need:
- coloured pencils

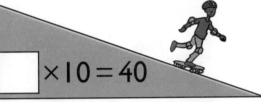

$\boxed{} \times 10 = 40$

$9 \times 10 = \boxed{}$

$\boxed{} \times 10 = 70$

$3 \times 10 = \boxed{}$

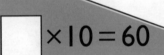

$\boxed{} \times 10 = 60$

$1 \times 10 = \boxed{}$

$\boxed{} \times 10 = 20$

$5 \times 10 = \boxed{}$

$\boxed{} \times 10 = 100$

$8 \times 10 = \boxed{}$

$\boxed{} \div \boxed{} = \boxed{}$ $\boxed{} \div \boxed{} = \boxed{}$ $\boxed{} \div \boxed{} = \boxed{}$

$\boxed{} \div \boxed{} = \boxed{}$ $\boxed{} \div \boxed{} = \boxed{}$

Teacher's notes

Complete each multiplication fact for 10 by writing the missing number into each space.
Then choose five of these and write the related division fact for each one. Colour them to match.

Date_____

Digger doubles

● **Know doubles of all numbers to 20**

You need:
● coloured pencils

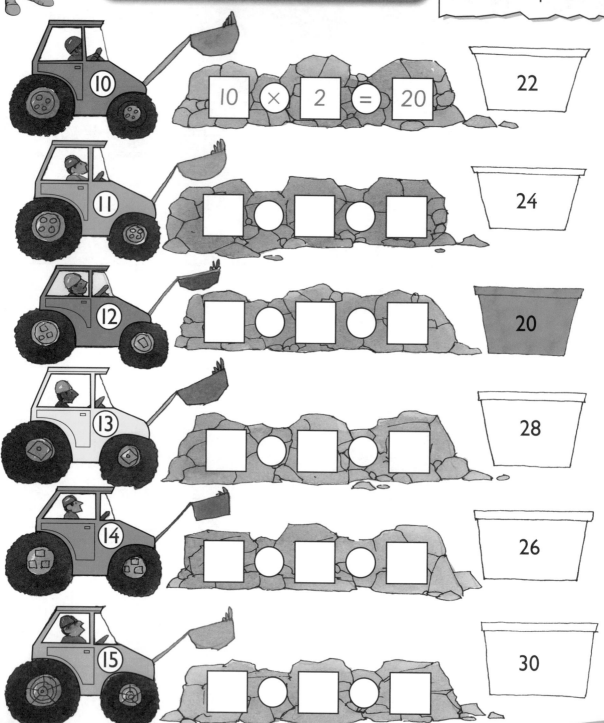

$10 \times 2 = 20$ — 22

24

20

28

26

30

Teacher's notes

Find the double of the number on each digger and write an addition or multiplication calculation in the spaces on the rubble. Colour the skip showing the same answer to match.

Date _____

Milky halves and doubles

● **Know doubles of all numbers to 20 and the matching halves**

Teacher's notes

Double the number on each cow and draw a line to join it to the milk carton showing the correct answer.
Now halve that number and colour the milkshake showing the correct answer to match.

Date _____

Fishy multiplication facts

● **Understand multiplication as an array**

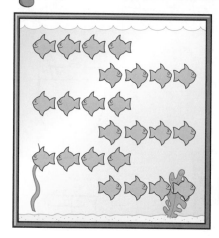

$$7 \times 2 = \boxed{}$$

$$9 \times 3 = \boxed{}$$

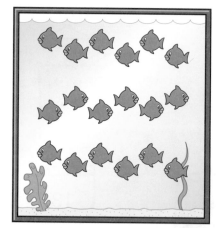

$$6 \times 4 = \boxed{}$$

$$8 \times 5 = \boxed{}$$

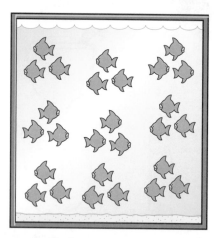

$$3 \times 6 = \boxed{}$$

$$2 \times 9 = \boxed{}$$

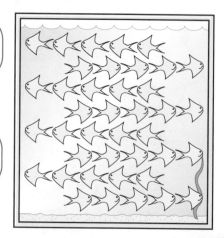

Teacher's notes

Look at the number of fish in each fish tank and then match each tank to the correct multiplication calculation. Complete the calculation.

Date _____

Sharing pears

● **Use arrays to understand multiplication and division**

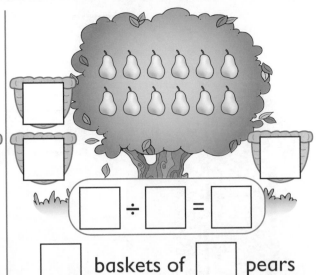

$10 \div 2 = 5$

☐ baskets of ☐ pears

☐ × ☐ = ☐

☐ ÷ ☐ = ☐

☐ baskets of ☐ pears

☐ × ☐ = ☐

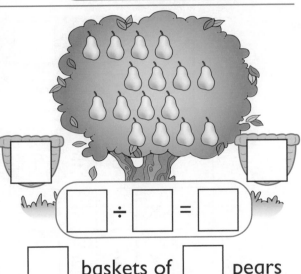

☐ ÷ ☐ = ☐

☐ baskets of ☐ pears

☐ × ☐ = ☐

☐ ÷ ☐ = ☐

☐ baskets of ☐ pears

☐ × ☐ = ☐

Teacher's notes

Look at the number of pears on each tree and then share them equally between the baskets underneath.
Write the corresponding division and multiplication number sentences in the spaces provided.

53

Date _____

Marvellous multiples

Know times table facts

×	1	2	3	4	5
1	1		3		5
2					
3					
4					
5					

☐ × 3 = 9   ☐ × 2 = ☐

3 × ☐ = ☐   4 × ☐ = ☐

☐ × 5 = ☐   ☐ × 5 = ☐

☐ × ☐ = ☐   ☐ × ☐ = ☐

Teacher's notes

54

Complete the multiplication grid by writing in the correct numbers.
Then use the grid to help you complete the number sentences and write two of your own.

Date _____

Number problems

● **Solve word problems**

There are 7 trees in the field.
There are 5 birds in each tree.

| 7 | × | 5 | = | 35 |

There are ☐ birds in the trees.

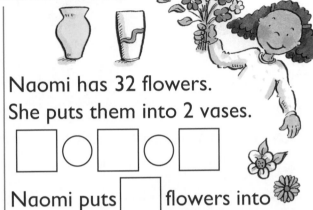

Naomi has 32 flowers.
She puts them into 2 vases.

☐ ◯ ☐ ◯ ☐

Naomi puts ☐ flowers into each vase.

Ellis has 3 shelves in his room.
Altogether there are 18 books.

☐ ◯ ☐ ◯ ☐

Ellis has ☐ books on
each shelf.

Mia has 2 boxes.
She tidies away 18 games
into each one.

☐ ◯ ☐ ◯ ☐

Mia has ☐ games altogether.

Tom bakes 8 cakes.
He puts 5 chocolate
buttons on each one.

☐ ◯ ☐ ◯ ☐

Tom uses ☐ chocolate
buttons.

There are 40 pencils
in each class.
They are shared equally
between 5 pots.

☐ ◯ ☐ ◯ ☐

There are ☐ pencils in
each pot.

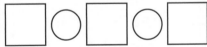

Teacher's notes
Look at each word problem and decide which number operation to use to work it out. Write the
appropriate calculation in the spaces provided.

Date _____

Creature calculations

● **Solve word problems**

There are tigers
sitting in 3 trees.
There are 5 tigers
in each tree.
How many tigers are there?

| 3 | ⊗ | 5 | = | |

Each tiger has 2 cubs.
How many tiger cubs
altogether?

| | ⊗ | | ○ | |

There are 3 prickly
pear cactii.
Each one has 18
prickly pears.
How many pears altogether?

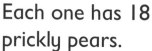

| | ○ | | ○ | |

3 bears eat all of
the prickly pears.
How many did each one eat

| | ○ | | ○ | |

There are 10 monkeys
eating fruit.
Altogether they eat
40 bananas.
How many bananas did
each monkey eat?

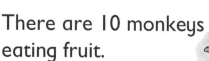

| | ○ | | ○ | |

The monkeys climb 5 trees.
How many are in each tree?

| | ○ | | ○ | |

There are birds in 4 trees.
There are 6 birds in
each tree.
How many birds are there?

| | ○ | | ○ | |

Each bird has laid 2 eggs.
How many eggs are
there altogether?

| | ○ | | ○ | |

Teacher's notes

Look at each word problem and decide which number operation to use to work it out.
Write the appropriate calculations in the spaces provided.

Date _____

Amazing multiplication

● Use symbols to record number sentences

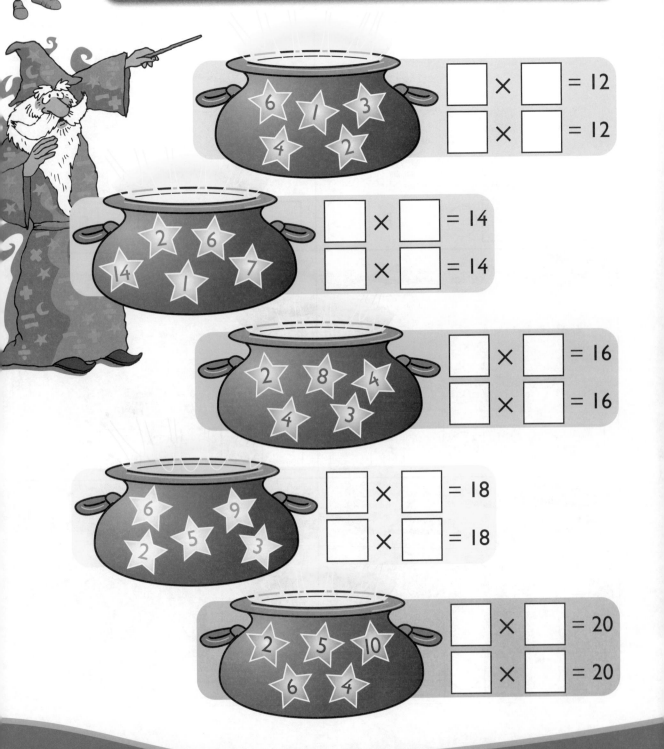

☐ × ☐ = 12
☐ × ☐ = 12

☐ × ☐ = 14
☐ × ☐ = 14

☐ × ☐ = 16
☐ × ☐ = 16

☐ × ☐ = 18
☐ × ☐ = 18

☐ × ☐ = 20
☐ × ☐ = 20

Teacher's notes

Complete each set of multiplication facts using the numbers in the cauldron next to them. Use each number only once, crossing off each one as it is used. There will be one number left in each cauldron.

Date _____

Rhino remainders

● **Understand the idea of remainders when dividing**

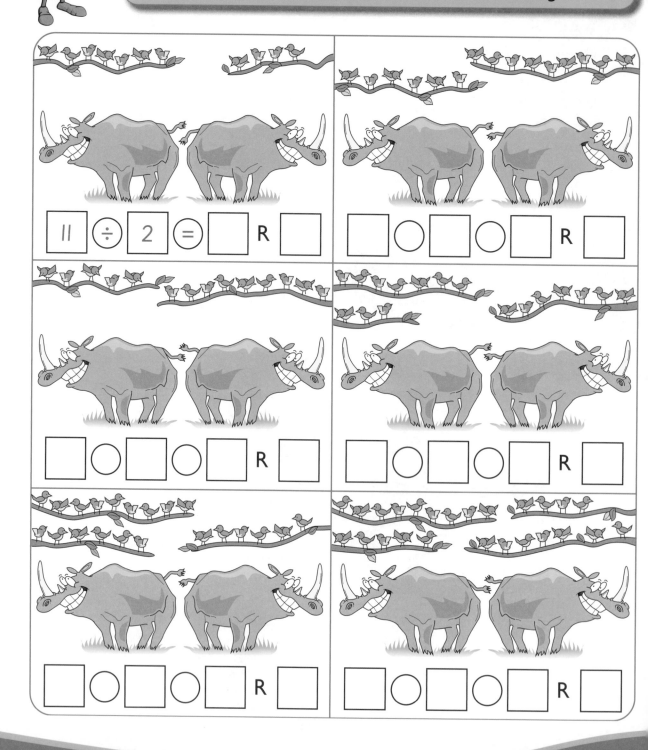

11 ÷ 2 = ☐ R ☐

☐ ○ ☐ ○ ☐ R ☐

☐ ○ ☐ ○ ☐ R ☐

☐ ○ ☐ ○ ☐ R ☐

☐ ○ ☐ ○ ☐ R ☐

☐ ○ ☐ ○ ☐ R ☐

Teacher's notes

58   Divide each group of birds equally between the rhinos. Write the correct division calculation underneath, including remainders where appropriate.

Date _____

Fairground solutions

● **Solve word problems**

Theo had 35p to spend on sticks of rock. Each cost 10p. How many sticks of rock could Theo buy?

20 people were queuing for the dodgems. There were 8 cars, and 2 people can fit in each one. How many people would have to wait for the *next* turn?

Ayesha bought 15 fizzers and 9 Pops. She shared them equally with Dan. How many sweets did they each have?

Joe had £5 and Kaya had £8. Ride tickets cost £2 each. How many tickets could they buy together?

Teacher's notes
Read each word problem and decide which operation to use to find out the answer.
You can use jottings and drawings to help you work it out and then write the calculation underneath.

Holiday halves

● Find one half of sets of objects

Teacher's notes

Top: Look at the number on each bucket. Colour each one to match the spade showing half of that number.
Bottom: Look at each pair of crabs. The number on the first crab is half of the number missing from the second crab. Write the missing number for each pair.

Date _____

Quarters 1, 2, 3

● **Find one quarter and three quarters of shapes and sets of objects**

You need:

● coloured pencils

Share each cake into quarters.
Colour the fraction shown under each one.

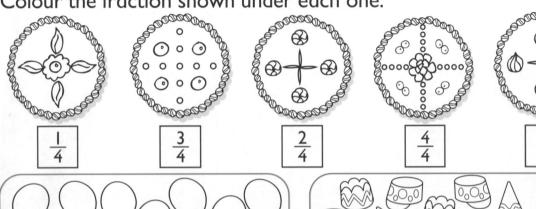

$\frac{1}{4}$　　$\frac{3}{4}$　　$\frac{2}{4}$　　$\frac{4}{4}$　　$\frac{1}{2}$

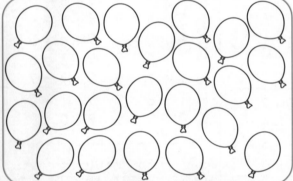

Colour one quarter
of the balloons.

Colour $\frac{3}{4}$ of these hats.

Colour two quarters
of these cakes.

Colour three quarters
of these presents.

Teacher's notes

Read the instructions for each picture, then colour as required to find one, two or three quarters of each object or set of objects.

61

Maths Facts

Number

0 1 2 3 4 5 6 7 8 9 10 11 12 13 14 15 16 17 18 19 20

Place value

100	200	300	400	500	600	700	800	900
10	20	30	40	50	60	70	80	90
1	2	3	4	5	6	7	8	9

Addition and subtraction facts to 10

0

$0 + 0 = 0$ $0 - 0 = 0$

1

$1 + 0 = 1$ $1 - 1 = 0$
$0 + 1 = 1$ $1 - 0 = 1$

2

$2 + 0 = 2$ $2 - 2 = 0$
$1 + 1 = 2$ $2 - 1 = 1$
$0 + 2 = 2$ $2 - 0 = 2$

3

$3 + 0 = 3$ $3 - 3 = 0$
$2 + 1 = 3$ $3 - 2 = 1$
$1 + 2 = 3$ $3 - 1 = 2$
$0 + 3 = 3$ $3 - 0 = 3$

4

$4 + 0 = 4$ $4 - 4 = 0$
$3 + 1 = 4$ $4 - 3 = 1$
$2 + 2 = 4$ $4 - 2 = 2$
$1 + 3 = 4$ $4 - 1 = 3$
$0 + 4 = 4$ $4 - 0 = 4$

5

$5 + 0 = 5$ $5 - 5 = 0$
$4 + 1 = 5$ $5 - 4 = 1$
$3 + 2 = 5$ $5 - 3 = 2$
$2 + 3 = 5$ $5 - 2 = 3$
$1 + 4 = 5$ $5 - 1 = 4$
$0 + 5 = 5$ $5 - 0 = 5$

6

$6 + 0 = 6$ $6 - 6 = 0$
$5 + 1 = 6$ $6 - 5 = 1$
$4 + 2 = 6$ $6 - 4 = 2$
$3 + 3 = 6$ $6 - 3 = 3$
$2 + 4 = 6$ $6 - 2 = 4$
$1 + 5 = 6$ $6 - 1 = 5$
$0 + 6 = 6$ $6 - 0 = 6$

7

$7 + 0 = 7$ $7 - 7 = 0$
$6 + 1 = 7$ $7 - 6 = 1$
$5 + 2 = 7$ $7 - 5 = 2$
$4 + 3 = 7$ $7 - 4 = 3$
$3 + 4 = 7$ $7 - 3 = 4$
$2 + 5 = 7$ $7 - 2 = 5$
$1 + 6 = 7$ $7 - 1 = 6$
$0 + 7 = 7$ $7 - 0 = 7$

8

$8 + 0 = 8$ $8 - 8 = 0$
$7 + 1 = 8$ $8 - 7 = 1$
$6 + 2 = 8$ $8 - 6 = 2$
$5 + 3 = 8$ $8 - 5 = 3$
$4 + 4 = 8$ $8 - 4 = 4$
$3 + 5 = 8$ $8 - 3 = 5$
$2 + 6 = 8$ $8 - 2 = 6$
$1 + 7 = 8$ $8 - 1 = 7$
$0 + 8 = 8$ $8 - 0 = 8$

9

$9 + 0 = 9$ $9 - 9 = 0$
$8 + 1 = 9$ $9 - 8 = 1$
$7 + 2 = 9$ $9 - 7 = 2$
$6 + 3 = 9$ $9 - 6 = 3$
$5 + 4 = 9$ $9 - 5 = 4$
$4 + 5 = 9$ $9 - 4 = 5$
$3 + 6 = 9$ $9 - 3 = 6$
$2 + 7 = 9$ $9 - 2 = 7$
$1 + 8 = 9$ $9 - 1 = 8$
$0 + 9 = 9$ $9 - 0 = 9$

10

$10 + 0 = 10$ $10 - 10 = 0$
$9 + 1 = 10$ $10 - 9 = 1$
$8 + 2 = 10$ $10 - 8 = 2$
$7 + 3 = 10$ $10 - 7 = 3$
$6 + 4 = 10$ $10 - 6 = 4$
$5 + 5 = 10$ $10 - 5 = 5$
$4 + 6 = 10$ $10 - 4 = 6$
$3 + 7 = 10$ $10 - 3 = 7$
$2 + 8 = 10$ $10 - 2 = 8$
$1 + 9 = 10$ $10 - 1 = 9$
$0 + 10 = 10$ $10 - 0 = 10$

Times table facts

1–100 number square

1	2	3	4	5	6	7	8	9	10
11	12	13	14	15	16	17	18	19	20
21	22	23	24	25	26	27	28	29	30
31	32	33	34	35	36	37	38	39	40
41	42	43	44	45	46	47	48	49	50
51	52	53	54	55	56	57	58	59	60
61	62	63	64	65	66	67	68	69	70
71	72	73	74	75	76	77	78	79	80
81	82	83	84	85	86	87	88	89	90
91	92	93	94	95	96	97	98	99	100

2 times table

$1 \times 2 = 2$	$6 \times 2 = 12$
$2 \times 2 = 4$	$7 \times 2 = 14$
$3 \times 2 = 6$	$8 \times 2 = 16$
$4 \times 2 = 8$	$9 \times 2 = 18$
$5 \times 2 = 10$	$10 \times 2 = 20$

5 times table

$1 \times 5 = 5$	$6 \times 5 = 30$
$2 \times 5 = 10$	$7 \times 5 = 35$
$3 \times 5 = 15$	$8 \times 5 = 40$
$4 \times 5 = 20$	$9 \times 5 = 45$
$5 \times 5 = 25$	$10 \times 5 = 50$

10 times table

$1 \times 10 = 10$	$6 \times 10 = 60$
$2 \times 10 = 20$	$7 \times 10 = 70$
$3 \times 10 = 30$	$8 \times 10 = 80$
$4 \times 10 = 40$	$9 \times 10 = 90$
$5 \times 10 = 50$	$10 \times 10 = 100$

Shape and space

2-D shapes

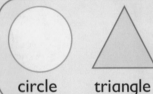 

circle   triangle   square   rectangle pentagon hexagon octagon

3-D solids

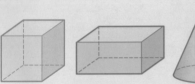

cube   cuboid   cone   cylinder   sphere   triangular-based pyramid   square-based pyramid

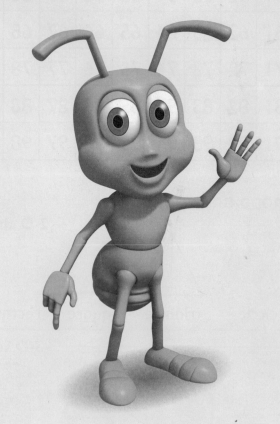

Collins
New
Primary
Maths

Published by Collins
An imprint of HarperCollins*Publishers*
77–85 Fulham Palace Road
Hammersmith
London
W6 8JB

Browse the complete Collins catalogue at
www.collinseducation.com

10 9 8 7 6 5 4 3

ISBN 978 0 00 722020 5

The authors assert their moral rights to be identified
as the authors of this work

British Library Cataloguing in Publication Data
A Catalogue record for this publication is available
from the British Library

Printed and bound by Printing Express, Hong Kong

ISBN 978-0-00-722020-5

Browse the complete Collins
Education catalogue at
www.collinseducation.com

9 780007 220205 >

2